Portraits of Grace

Phyllis A Comeaux

Pebbles to Gold Publishing Company

Copyright © 2015-2023 Phyllis A Comeaux

ISBN: 979-8-9857039-4-8

DEDICATION

This book of poems is dedicated with much love to all my children, Michelle, David, and Julie; their spouses, Jon, Desirée and Trevor; and all my grandchildren, Lily and Zoë, Autumn and Natalie, and Emmitt and Meyer and baby brother on the way, as they learn to love and grow in love with the Holy Trinity through their own journey during quiet prayer time. The journey can be quite exhilarating if you can quiet your soul, wait and listen. And to my husband, John, who has lived the journey with me and patiently watches as it unfolds.

I would also like to dedicate this book to my Godmother, Mary Theriot, who has received a copy of nearly every poem in the book, mostly inspired to be written for her as they gave her so much joy. She was a special gift to me and I will always treasure our relationship.

CONTENTS

Portraits of Grace

ACKNOWLEDGMENTS

I would like to thank all of those who have helped to nurture this endeavor along the way, even before any aspiration of it becoming a book. So first, I must acknowledge the St Joseph Abbey Retreat Center and the wonderful Archbishop, monks, priests and support staff who have made my annual retreat for over 10 years a very rich and growth filled experience. Not to mention that my very first poem was inspired on the Abbey grounds in 2015 and several poems thereafter, as the setting and silence allowed me to hear the still small voice of the spirit. When I finally let someone read it, Br Ephraim encouraged me to keep writing, so I have not stopped.

I would also like to acknowledge the ACTS retreats and prayer groups that I have been involved in since my first retreat in 2016. Once again, the Spirit speaks in many ways and through my prayer group, I have also been encouraged and some of the poems were inspired by different people and situations.

I must also acknowledge another very influential individual in my adult faith formation, Ashton Mouton, who looked at this timid little creature and saw in her heart a love for the Faith and a desire to grow. He somehow managed to nudge and encourage in a way that I could not refuse, so I became involved in so many ministries at church under his pastoral care. We met up again for coffee one day, and I showed him some of my poems and he too encouraged me to keep writing and to share them.

And most importantly, I would like to acknowledge, my most enthusiastic supporter, John, who has patiently read and offered suggestions, edits on many of these poems which truly helped to improve them and I value his input so much because he is an excellent writer and editor. And I thank him for his encouragement, his patience and time in helping this come together for my family.

INTRODUCTION

This particular set of writing consists of personal messages and poems given to me from the Holy Spirit during intimate prayer time over the past seven years. The very first one came to me while attending my annual December retreat at St Joseph's Abbey in Covington, LA. It happened to be a little over 4 months after my mother's passing and the title "Humility" says it all. I wrote the first half of it in about 20 minutes while sitting outdoors on a bench in the cool fall weather, enjoying the peace while still grieving my mother's passing. I had never really written poetry before, so the beauty and perfection of it amazed me and I knew it was divinely inspired. The Spirit has marvelous ways of healing. The first four verses came quickly and gave me a sense of peace. But I had to stop to attend Sunday mass, and from there the retreat schedule quickly came to a close and life moved on.

As much as I thought about it afterwards, nothing else was inspired. Until about 6 months later, sitting in my prayer chair after a time of meditation, I picked it up and the rest of the poem flowed out in perfection. There were no scratch outs, alterations… The entire poem was obviously given to me by the Holy Spirit word for word and I obliged the reception by recording it and was very humbled by the whole occurrence.

From that time, I journaled quite a bit during/after my meditation time. But it was several more years before the poems started to flow. I was always very fond of my Godmother, but after my Mom passed, she became my earthly maternal love. I had always felt close to her, but that love grew as time went by. It seemed to bring her such joy when I brought her a new poem that was inspired by prayer or adoration. So I secretly wished the Spirit would inspire me during that time – and He came through for me.

She was taken to her Heavenly home at the age of 92, this past March, 2023. And I do believe this Holy Spirit was giving us both a gift as the poems came more and more frequently, so I never went to visit without a new poem, once or twice a week.

My journaling continues and may one day lead to another book as there is often quite a bit of imagery. But for now, I wish for my family to share this book and the deep connection I have with our great God, His Son, Jesus and the Holy Spirit as well as the Blessed Mother. I pray always for the grace to do His will and for all of my family, friends and those in most need of Divine Intervention.

At the end of the spiritual section are 7 poems for my grandchildren, starting with "My Easter Lily".

Phyllis Comeaux, 2023

Portraits of Grace

HUMILITY

The Winds blow, the Times change, the Spirit moves
The roaring of the Wind through the Trees
The crashing of the Waves in the Sea
The Falling of the leaves; Trunks bare and naked
The moving of the Tide flowing in and out.

So the Spirit comes in full force
A breath of Wind that knocks us off our feet
Or a whisper, faint and barely audible
Did I hear you, Lord? Are you there?
Please, I pray, let me know you are here.

And again the Spirit comes as a Tidal Wave
Moving things great and small—changing them forever
Cleansing and purging all that needs to go
Leaving behind only the foundation that is true
Humility—the Basis of Conversion

The Winter comes and the nights grow long
The sun is shy, hiding its face, guarding its light
There is little comfort in the dark and cold of winter
Just like the trees, I am bare, naked and alone
Humility—moves the soul in a new direction

The tide flows in, the smooth glassy sea
Calm and peace in perfect rhythm
Beware turbulence, disparity below
The tide flows out, revealing what is hidden
Humility—exposes the heart

Portraits of Grace

Open heart, inside-out
Vulnerable, emptied of itself
Reaching out for what is True
Finding Love and giving too
Man, Woman, Father, Son
The Spirit unifies as One
Humility—the bond of true Love

Humility, a journey through Life
Moving towards perfection and Light
Binding relationships along the Way
Discovering the Mystery of the Trinity
Humility—unity, love and harmony

Retreat December 2015

HOPE

The seed is planted
The soil is watered
Rays of sunshine nurture life
The little seedling peeks through the earth
Hope is born awaiting the blossom
The fruits of new life—BEAUTY

Love attracts
The two become one
God's grace nurtures their union
A child is conceived within the womb
Hope is awaiting the birth
The fruit of God's creation—LOVE

Washed clean by tears from the sky
Falling upon the wayward people
A smile appears amongst the remnant droplets
Though upside down, the shape of a frown
Hope abounds in its radiant colors
The fruit of the promise—FORGIVENESS

The tree that once bore life
Now stands against the dark sky
Bearing the Word that spoke all creation
Now covered in blood, tears and humility
Hope is present in the promise of new life—the Resurrection
The fruit of the cross—MERCY

Portraits of Grace

A step onto the path
Meandering through the lush greenery
Anticipating a breathtaking view around every curve
Emerging in a clearing under the golden sun
Hope arises as the glassy lake displays its reflected beauty
The fruit of the journey—PEACE

November 2019

THE LOVE OF MY LIFE
(And Beyond)

As the Spirit moves, there is little warning
A whisper, a feeling, a huge jolt
That knocks me down and changes things forever
Run as I may, I can never get away
The senses are heightened, awareness grows
Your love surrounds me and then overflows
It draws me in like a huge ocean tide
That takes me on an ecstatic ride

In the days of love and roses
My heart would skip a beat
Longing to gaze into your eyes
Filled with gentleness and compassion
Yearning for your tender kiss
A brush upon my lips
The anticipation of the encounter
As I hurry to our meeting place
My prayer chair awaits

First, you did prepare me, by shedding of my skin
Naked before you, contrite and humble I stand
Receiving your robe of white, after pardon of my sin
I am ready for the most perfect intimate union
As I receive your body into mine thru Holy Communion
We shall come together in perfect harmony
Until my human nature stains the robe again
But the shedding of your blood takes away the sin
My robe is clean, once more

Portraits of Grace

You gave me gifts of great treasure,
Meaning so much more than simple pleasure
Promises of love eternal, growing day by day
Nurturing little by little in your tender caring way
Sending rays of light streaming thru the trees
Highlighting magnificent colors of turning Autumn leaves
Wrapping lustrous pearl in your words of wisdom
Drawing me ever closer to your promised Kingdom

The days of courting long gone now
My heart is yours forever
As you have engraved your name upon it
I pray it beats in synchrony with yours
And though I run and frolic
Thru fields of golden grain
I am going to meet Our Father
Who has called me by my name
He has special work for me to do
Sowing seeds and gathering too
Mending fences, shedding tears
Letting go of all my fears

As we grow old together, the flame is less ablaze
And we are just content with a quiet knowing gaze
We often sit in silence, exchanging not a word
But with warmth, love and passion, we are far from being
bored

The days are drawing closer when our betrothal will be known
And my bridegroom will announce He is calling me home
My wedding gown will be adorned, the most dazzling white
Never to be stained again as He stands on my right
Presenting me to Our Father for His Blessing of Eternal Light

December 2019

THE JOY OF YOU

Fill me with the joy of You
Like You never have before
Away with all the sorrows
For You have borne it all.

"Be still", you say, "Sit with Me"
I want to draw you near
Open your heart, let me in
Love will fill your soul

Fear and anxiety fall away
Your comfort takes its place
Peace is all around me
As you fill me with Your grace.

The corners of my heart
Once hidden, dark and dingy
Now turned inside-out
Emptied of all its misery
Become alive with the Essence of You
Reflecting the Light of Your love and glory

Fill me with the joy of You
Like you never have before
Drawing me close all the time
I come to You once more

March 2020

BUBBLE

Floating in a bubble
All along the Way
Protect me from this Virus
Every single Day

Surround me with your Spirit
For fear is everywhere
No matter where I turn
Looms isolation and despair
And I think of You with sorrow and
The Cross You had to bear
And I remember the hope
that You came to share

So I turn my heart to Your Cross
To show me the way
to overcome the loss and feelings of strife
Your Spirit surrounds me in my state of dismay
And comforts me with Peace, Love and Joy
That soothe throughout the day
Turning the mourning into gladness at the promise of Life

March 2020

EPIPHANY POEM

In the shadows of my eyes,
As though hidden in the trees,
I catch a glimpse of You
Looking directly at me.

As the leaves begin to glisten
From Your light and inner glow,
You emerge from the darkness
With your hands stretched out so.

I see the marks from the nails
And I shudder in dismay,
As I recognize the consequences
Of the part I had to play.

I bury my face in shame
For the sin that caused such pain
But You lift my chin towards You
As You whisper, "it was all for your gain."

I am overcome by the love
That flows from every pore,
Washing gently over me
And cleansing me once more.

Your forgiveness is everlasting
Your love is without bounds
Now I must go forward
Proclaiming Your love with resound.

Filled with Love and peace
I rush out into the streets
With joy, singing Your praises
To each and every soul I meet.

My time with You is precious
As I search for You in prayer;
Through times of light and darkness,
I know You're always there.

We will never be apart
Even in times of desolation;
And that alone gives me peace
And a sense of consolation.

January 2021

CHILD OF MARY

A child of God
So meek and so mild
Born of the Spirit
For Love divine
Open to the Will of the Father
Bearing sorrows as did Our Mother
She is a Child of Mary

Filled with words of truth and wisdom
Reaching out to spread Good News
Working tirelessly for salvation of souls
Comforting others with compassion and mercy
Soothing fears, spreading hope
Loving all—even His foes
He is a Child of Mary

Strong and confident in her faith
Never wavering from the truth
Seeking love, but giving more
Filled with concern for those around her
She has a deep inner strength
That gives support to those in need
She is a Child of Mary

Driven towards seeking perfection
Searching for the lost and lonely
Humility is the essence of His being
That softens His poignant manner
As He reaches into the depths of my soul
To draw out the truth before my eyes
He is a Child of Mary

April 2021

THE SHEPHERD AND THE LAMB

The Shepherd comes to call His sheep
Each and every one by name
He tends to their every need
And heals those who are lame

The Shepherd shows them love and kindness
For He has come to lead the Way
To luscious pastures, flowing waters
Going after those who stray.

And yet, His greatest act of love
Is to give His life for His sheep
So through the grace of Heaven above
He's willingly led to the slaughter
As the pure and unblemished lamb
A gift of atonement to the Father.

He does not fight, nor bleat, nor run away
As he's led to the cross of sacrifice
Stretching arms out on that fateful day
Receiving the sword that took His life.

This Lamb, so perfect and pure
Also the Shepherd that gives His all
To keep His sheep out of the brambles
Receiving those thorns into His skull

January 2021

PEACE OF THE LORD

Longing and desire fill my every breath
As I kneel in Your Presence
Praying for your Peace to wash over me,
Fill me, surround me, captivate me
Or just let me have a brief encounter
To keep me going til I am breathless once more.

And suddenly, it begins—a vision of Your Peace
As it washes over me, a sea of blue
That comes to rest so still and tranquil
I dare not move to make even a ripple in this perfect Peace
And as I continue to gaze upon the sea,
It appears that a dove of Peace has glided upon the sea
So brilliant, so white, so perfect
As it spreads its wings far and wide over the waters
Like a blanket holding in the peace so it can't escape

But the Peace of the Lord is so great
That it cannot be contained
It must be released, to be spread far and wide, and as it does,
The brilliance of the white covering becomes even greater,
almost blinding as it rises to the Heavens
And I realize that the Glory of God accompanies that Peace
And what a Gift it is to behold.

July 2021

SOUND OF SILENCE

Quietly waiting, I sit
Aware of the darkness and silence
Eyes closed; ears perked
For the hint of a sound
Or a glimmer of light
SILENCE

What appears in the darkness
Is not light, but a red blob
The color of His blood
As the small circle spreads
It washes over me
Showering me with graces of
MERCY

He has captured me once again
Saving me from the destruction of my sin
Not yet aware, I had gone astray
He rescues me in a subtle way
Pointing me in a new direction
Leaving no room for indiscretion
HOPE

Out of bondage, I am free
He sets my sails so not to drift
Never to roam or be alone
His hand on mine will ever be
My most cherished gift
HUMILITY

Rise from prayer, go on my way
He will be with me through the day
No need to fear nor to wonder
What will happen if things go asunder
His WILL be mine, and all will be fine
FAITH

January 2022

COME TO ME

Lord,
Come to me in the quiet of the night
Come to me in the noise of the day
Come to me in my inner soul
Awaken my spirit whenever I pray

Put away my troubles and fright
Let me focus on all that is right
Finding words is not desired
Opening my heart is what's required

Let your Spirit take over
And fill every crack
Mend what is broken
Then give my heart back

Renewed and refreshed
The blood begins to flow
I know I am blessed
You have told me so

My heart begins to swell
Until it's ready to burst
And the love overflows
Who'll receive it first?

The ones You have chosen
Who come into my sight
Will receive this gift of love
Crowned with everlasting light

Portraits of Grace

January 2022

MY ANGEL

My Godmother, my Angel
Little do you know
How much you've meant to me
From now, thru days of long ago

Even as a young child
I felt the bond of love
Special as that of a Godmother
Blessed by Heaven above

Growing and becoming confirmed
I chose Mary as my name
Loving both our Heavenly Mother
And the Faith you kept without shame

You are always so kind and caring
Such a blessing to me you have been
Praying, laughing and sharing
I treasure you as a friend
I love to come and visit
Spending time with you again

You greet me always so special
With a twinkle in your eye
And a smile across your face
A gentle kiss on the head
As so fondly we embrace

Portraits of Grace

You squeeze my hand in yours
Holding it ever so tight
And we become one
Bound in Spirit and Light

I pray for you always
May the Lord keep you and Bless you
And hold you close to His heart
With Mother Mary by your side
May we never be apart
My Godmother, my Angel

February 2022

LIT BY YOUR MIGHTY HAND

Like a burning candle
I desire to be
Lit by Your mighty hand
In great kindness to me
Losing shape and form
The longer I burn
No one other than you
Would recreate and not spurn

This flowing sea of wax
You look upon with kindness
And in your love and mercy
You do not see a mess
But find in me potential
To become something else
Besides an unattractive blob
Of hardened useless wax

You scoop this molten sea
Into your warm and gentle hands
To keep me soft and pliable
To use for your great plans
You mold me in a whole new shape
And by adding in some color bands
An inner beauty you give to me
That pleases you for eternity

Portraits of Grace

The final piece that is the key
The wick that comes from You
And runs straight through me
The one that you will light
From the fire in your heart
Starting in me a fire of love
So that we are never apart

You are the light of the world
Spreading from one to another
Shining before man through the ages
Making us one with you and our brother
Come Holy Spirit, light my fire
A sea of wax to a candle of love
Lit by Your mighty hand
Reaching down from Heaven above

March 2022

A NEW SONG

Create in me a new song
A melody with Heavenly aura
That surrounds me with grace
Lifts my spirit to new heights
With a crescendo that
Bursts into the fullness of resonance
With all of Your creation

Allow the music of Heaven
To penetrate my soul as
The sharp notes poke and prod me on
To stretch my ears
To the sound of Your call
 Impose the flats to dampen my will
Which tend to serve <u>my</u> desires over Yours

Let the movements of my spiritual life
flow from one to another with mystical grace
So that the discord in my life
is converted to sweet sounds
And the final refrain which repeats
Is of harmony deep in my soul
Filling me with peace in every measure
And the stream of Heavenly music
Becomes the new song of my life

June 2022

POURING GRACES

The Sun is shining brightly
As its rays stream down to Earth
Spreading out its graces
To bring us to rebirth

The clouds gather round it
All fluffy, big and white
Beckoning us towards Heaven
And the One true source of light

But then, the light begins to fade
As the clouds turn shades of gray
And my fear begins to grow, as
Without the Son, my path may go astray

Then the clouds begin to weep
Sending drops to hidden places
And I realize that the Son
Is pouring down special graces

I skip and run between the drops
Filled with relief and pure delight
As the Son will always shine upon me
With His true love and perfect light

(about my prayer life)
Abbey Retreat December 2021

RING OF FIRE

Surround me, Lord
With a ring of Fire
Burn away rubbish
Light the Way
As my needs at this time
are becoming dire

The flames shooting outward from the ring
Will protect me from harm
To my inner being
And those shooting inward
Toward my soul
Will convict my heart
To depths untold

Lighting a fire of passion
To serve you more
Reaching out to my neighbor
And opening doors
While burning away
The thistles and thorns
That poke and distract
And leave me forlorn

Yes, a ring of fire
Is what I need
Dispelling the darkness
So that I may be freed
Bringing Light to those
Who are lost, indeed
Guiding them away
From judgment and greed

Showing them the love
In Your ring of fire
Brilliant with Your radiant glory
Filling them all with great desire
To draw closer to You
As with the lure of a lyre
Surround us Lord with
Your alluring Ring of Fire

July 2022

IN ADORATION

Behold the Majestic Presence
That captures the heart and soul
With rays of glory and splendor as
They emanate in every direction
Reaching out to all of Creation
That You have spoken into being

You are the Lord of the Universe
Ruler of the World
Lover of all creatures great and small
Providing Your love and protection
Keeping us safe as You heed our call
To protect us from a tragic fall

Pouring out graces as You sense their prayer
Landing on those who reach out to You
Letting them fill the empty heart
With comfort and blessings
That stir their senses
As love, joy and peace
Overcome their being

And their eyes are opened
To see the King of Creation
Holding out the Lamb of Salvation
As an offering to each and every one
Who humbly desires to receive
The Most precious gift of all

And I bow my head and torso
In homage before Your Majesty
Grateful for every day
That you offer Yourself to me
In Eucharistic Celebration
As well as precious time
In Adoration
My Jesus
My Savior
My Love

August 2022

THE FIRE OF YOUR LOVE

Holy Spirit, come to me
To enkindle my heart
With the fire of Your love
Set my heart ablaze
To burn away the rubbish
As the flames leap and dance
From one dead spot to another
Turning sin and indifference
To a pile of ash
Stirring it into something
That will last

As the smoldering, unrecognizable
Are showered with the water of Your graces
And mixed by the strength of Your wings
As You swoop through
The interior of my heart
Purging the old, making it new
Enriching this inner sanctum
Making it suitable for You
And the new growth that You have foreseen
That will become a reality
And not just a dream
As the walls of my heart
Burn with desire
To hold the fire of Your love
For the world to see
Spreading it to others for Eternity

October 2022

30

LOVE BORN OF BLOOD

As I kneel before your precious body
I close my eyes to catch a glimpse
Of the Sacred Heart I love so dearly;
And coming forth towards my heart
Is a bloody hand with a gaping hole
Reaching forward deep into my soul
The one that once nailed to the cross
Was pierced to save all who are lost

I hear Your voice as you whisper to me
You must bare your soul for all to see
That I may caress your heart so tenderly
And coax the flow of life-giving blood
Into a torrent of love much like a flood
That seeps into nooks and crevices
Wearing away sharp, hurtful edges

And as it does, the stream slows its pace
Gently flowing, filled with love and grace
Amid drops of blood that you shed for me
Reminding me to love for all eternity
Those You have put into my loving care
And teaching them also that they must share
The love and peace that comes their way
With those around them every day

July 2022

THE SPIRIT OF GOD

Third person of the Trinity
Though not the least of all three
Mostly hidden from sight
Has ways of reaching us
Changing us, Shaping us
As we learn of His might
Through many forms we come to know
The powers He bears and can bestow

A gift of God, precious as a gem
Multifaceted, radiating such brilliance
As we uncover the beauty within
We must open our hearts to the **gifts** He bears
Allowing us the **wisdom** to judge what is truth
And come to **know him** and **understand**
And grow in that knowledge of Him and
His path that leads to eternal salvation

In the silence of our heart,
Our 'spirits' are joined as we become friends
And He gives us good **counsel** and a glimpse of God
To help us grow strong with firmness of mind
For doing good and avoiding evil
Filling us with love that knows no bounds
That we can share with those all around
He teaches us **Piety**, as we worship the Father
And hold firm to the path that led the Way
As all of the Saints did with fervor each day

From where comes the sound
that makes us yearn
And search all around
it's hard to discern

Portraits of Grace

A whisper so gentle and quiet
Words of the Spirit, is it just a whim
Or a voice so loud and clear
I am not certain, could it be Him

I look around to see who's near
Finding no one, my heart skips a beat
Don't panic, be still and shed no tear
The Spirit of God is the sound you hear
In humble silence, we must be aware
Of the message from God that He has to share
So listen my child and don't be afraid
Though the Spirit is mighty, He's also my friend

For **Fear of the Lord** is a gift
That binds you to Him so you cannot drift
In reverence and respect
We Hold Him in awe
As we praise, worship and adore
The One we will love forevermore

Though not possible to see before your eyes
His presence is known by the sound of His call
To the depths of your heart in His subtle way
That protects you from a treacherous fall
So with **Fortitude** we stand firm
Drawing closer and closer, fearing separation
Thanking God for the bearer of these precious gifts
United to us at our Confirmation

The Holy Spirit is alive in us
If we let Him into our every endeavor
May the Spirit be with you
Now and forever

January 2023

IN THE DARKNESS

My Jesus, my love, I come to You
Longing to feel Your love so true
To hear Your voice, to feel Your touch
I have missed You so very much

You have taught me through Your Saints
To persevere and not grow faint
For in the darkness there is light
Radiating from joy through inner sight
Accepting the void in humility
As you once did as you hung on a tree
My God, my god, why have You forsaken me
A cry of despair, ending in death
Leading to Glory and Life for all eternity

The rays of warmth that permeate the soul
Cannot be felt or sensed in the dark of night
But Faith and trust from knowledge of You
Collected and cherished in hours of prayer
Have laid the cornerstone for me to bear
The loss I feel in the stillness of time
Until once more my prayer is sublime
To have and to hold forever more
Deep in my heart as in days of yore

Til deep in the desert I hear a voice
Are You the one I have been waiting for
And a rush of love flows through me
As I sense the day of victory
Being lifted up on angels' wings

Portraits of Grace

With a heavenly voice that I may sing
Praise for perseverance and trust in You
To return to me, forever more
The love of my life, my love so true
Out of darkness, I come to You

On Retreat
December 2022

MY PRAYER

Come to me, Jesus
Send Your Spirit
To open my heart
To expand my mind
To let my ears hear
To put words in my mouth
To prepare my hands
That I may do Your work
And love more

Fill me with Your essence
Fill me with Your being
Fill me with Your love
Fill me with Your patience
Fill me with Your compassion
That I may love more
And do Your will

Remove all my selfishness
Take away my self-centeredness
Destroy my pridefulness
Decrease my ungodly desires
Reform my daily priorities
To match those You have for me
That I may do Your will
And become Your faithful servant

Make me an instrument of Your Peace
Teach me more about humility
Give me a servant heart
Touch my tongue with Words of Wisdom
Encourage my hands to reach out to others
That I may be Your faithful servant
And bring others closer to You

Let me listen to their needs
Let me fill them with Your love
Let me show them Your mercy
Let me share with them Your peace
Let me help heal their wounds
That they may become closer to You
And love You the way I want to
With all my heart, mind and soul

Come to me, Jesus, I pray
AMEN

January 2023

HIDDEN FROM SIGHT

I close my eyes
And search for You
But try as I might
There is nothing I do
That lets in the light
So You come into view
Hidden from sight
I have no glimpse of You

Sit back and be still
I hear in my mind
What happens is My will
With no effort of thine
Except to open your heart
That lets My light shine
And fill it with warmth
Of My love divine

So together we sit
In the silence of prayer
And I move not a bit
Knowing that You are there
I feel my heart swell
Being filled to the brim
Ready to explode
With the essence of Him

The joy is immense
The love is so deep
The peace like a blanket
That has no end
But wraps all around
The two of us within
Hidden from sight
May it never end

January 2023

JESUS, BE IN ME

Dear Jesus, I pray
That you come to me every day
Fill my heart with Your love
Even BE my heart from Heaven above
That soars with wings like a dove
Filled with grace and precious love

BE my eyes to see the need
That continues to grow fueled by greed
Of those who keep all to themselves
The surplus that could certainly be shared
By each of those who truly cared

BE my hands to do the work
That builds the Kingdom brick by brick
With blood, sweat, passion or tears
And prayers, grace and a lack of fear
So that the final result looks like the plan
That you had in mind before the fall of Man

BE my tongue that spreads the Word
Echoing the prophets with a double-edged sword
Who slashed many falsehoods in days of yore
While presenting the truths surrounded in glory
That shed its light on all human history
With the promise of salvation as the final story

Portraits of Grace

BE my ears that hear the Father
As He guides me on the Way
To be with Him and never falter
Doing His will throughout the day
Then finding time to sit and pray
Listening to the voice that bids me to stay
Resting in peace at the end of the day

BE my feet that walk Your Way
The Way of the Cross every day
Accepting the trials that come along
As I walk and stumble over rocky ground
Or climb up a hill being stoned by a throng
When finally, through the mist You are found
Always BE in every part of ME
Every word and every deed
Consoling others and filling needs
Giving love, Finding joy
Loving life, never annoyed
Content forever with what IS
According to Your Will
I let it BE—in Me

January 2023

A GARDEN OF LIFE

First and foremost, the center of love in your life
Was the God who gave grace to see you through strife
You were born for His love, given to share
As you bore child after child and gave motherly care
To the gifts he bestowed and the challenge you bore
That made you rely on His love and forgiveness that much
more

Each of these gifts were tiny little seeds
That needed protection from the bad weeds
Cultivated by His angels and cherished so dear
Each of these seeds grew year after year
Fed with the fertilizer of Love everlasting
and watered with His Grace, another blessing

So, the garden blossomed and grew, spreading seeds all around
With stories of gladness or sadness worked into the ground
And God watched as you nurtured everything you've sown
And looks with pleasure on all that you have grown
Yes, some have wilted and died, but He's taken them home
To a place where they flourish, and are never alone
Waiting to see you, love you and join you as one

And the love and tender care
that you poured out all your life,
day after day in spite of some strife
Is a tribute to you as a mother and wife
A breathtakingly beautiful garden
Maybe not perfect, but no need for pardon

As God of the Universe, deep in your heart
Smiles upon you and your garden of Life
With you forever as death will not part
A garden <u>He</u> created from the very start
A Garden of Love
Everlasting

January 2023

A NEW DAWN

Like the lunar pull in the dark of night
A welling begins in the depths of my heart
It seems to grow to a certain degree
Then subsides as it slowly departs from me
And the sea of my soul is still and cold
As I dream of the dawn when I behold
The movement that stirs deep in my soul

With hope in my heart, I wait for the morn
Much as the world did when the savior was born
I will not know of the place or the time
But wait I must, for His will is mine
I dare not be idle, but do what I can
To share what He's taught me
And give praise for His plan

The darkness lingers as I yearn for the tide
To flow in once again and <u>never</u> subside
But this will not happen, I know without doubt
That as the Spirit moves, it flows in and out
And in the low tide, that leaves my soul bare
I must look for the treasures that He gives me to share
The pearls in the shells that peek out from the sand
Looking rough and foreboding, but holding beauty within

As the Son rises over the deep blue sea
And wave of peace washes over me
Emerging from the clouds in brilliant rays
The light of His glory warms my soul
And replaces the darkness that felt so cold

For ages it seemed it would never end
But now I know a new day will begin
As the Spirit moves in rhythmic waves
A new dawn will come for all to praise

January 2023

A MOTHER'S HEART

We look to Mary, our perfect guide
On mothering our children
Throughout their lives
A tender heart filled with love
Adorned with Grace from Heaven above
Beaming with joy as her little ones grow
Pierced with sadness at times we won't know
But accepting God's will is the only way
To shoulder the burden and get through the day

Mary, our Mother and model of prayer
We follow her example, if we dare
Praying unceasingly from the very start
To shelter and guide their little hearts
In a world whose influence can do such harm
And draw them away from our loving arms
To a place of darkness and deceptive charm
But do not despair and become all teary
Just pray little mother and do not grow weary

As you teach and encourage, they will grow and flourish
While you clean and cook and constantly nourish
Their little bodies grow strong and their hearts know love
As you also teach about Heaven above
And show by example the peace of a dove
Keeping and pondering on what's in your mind
As they wander off and sometimes out of line

Worry and stress will present its face
But always remember to ask for God's grace
And ask our dear Mother to help and to guide
So that you and your children will not collide
The life of a family can be quite a ride

But more often than not
You will be bursting with pride
As you watch them grow
in faith, love and charity
And you will think back to those days
When you were lacking clarity
And thank Mother Mary when you kneel to pray
As your heart is at peace at least for today

January 2023

THE DANCE

We take our places from the beginning
And look at our partner eye to eye
Curtsy to you, bow to me
Hand in hand, the music starts
And I treasure this time deep in my heart
As we dance and swirl to the rhythms of life
Sometimes in step and other times not
But keeping time just the same
As we keep moving to the end of the song

There are different songs that are part of the dance
Some that have a change of pace
Or maybe those we have not danced to before
So we must follow the lead of the hand we hold
And pray it's the one that will keep the time
So we don't stumble and fall as others watch
But stay nimble on our feet with grace and respect
For the teacher of the dance and the music of our lives

Some songs are slow and easy, moving with a flow
Like waves in the water that go to and fro
Swaying and enjoying the look in your eyes
That goes deep into my soul and skips in my heart
Others are fast with a changing beat
that keeps us on our toes as we maneuver on the floor
Breathless and frantic we come to the end
Thankful that we made it without falling apart
Laughing at the creator and wonder at His purpose
But joyful that we made it to the end of that song

Portraits of Grace

One day we will hear the very last song
The dance will be over and the day will be done
It will finally be time for us to go home
To our Father in Heaven for He is the one
Who gave us the tickets to be part of the dance
And sent His Spirit to chaperone
While His Son was our teacher from day one
And you were my partner from the very first dance

February 2023

WISDOM

Wisdom is a woman beguiling all
To whom She graces Her presence
Alluring and graceful are the words of HER mouth
Yet poignant and piercing to the depths of my heart
She knows me inside and out
Today Her words are of peace and comfort
And tomorrow they pierce my inner soul
Revealing what is hidden from my conscience
As my shame finds its way to the surface

What, O Wisdom, am I to do
As I turn to hide my face from you
There is no escape for She is always there
As the beginning of Wisdom comes from God
Who brought Her into being before creation
And the Word of God was with Wisdom
As He created the Heavens and the Earth
Her beauty is as transient as the day or the night
At times hidden in darkness or as brilliant as light

Today She is clothed in soft words of peace
With a veil of comfort that She nestles over me
I draw close to Her as She whispers in my ear
The sentiments that allay all of my fear
But tomorrow She may come surrounded by fire
To burnish the thoughts of my selfish desires
Or smoke out the pride that won't let me rest
As I veer off on a path that leads me astray
From one I should be on each and every day

O Wisdom, come and be my friend
Let me not be afraid to hear what you have to say
For I know the eyes of my heart are blinded at times
So that your beauty seems elusive as I struggle to pray
For the understanding that you want to give me today
Let my eyes be opened and my ears hear
The message that you whisper in words loud and clear
That startles my soul with a lightning bolt
Or soothes my spirit with peace and with hope

February 2023

GIVE GLORY

Give glory to God the Father
Who is illuminated by all of creation
Especially the natural beauty of the world
And all of its wonders therein
Also, by the beings He created
Who have chosen to draw close to Him
As they reflect the love of the Father
As well as the light within
Which intensifies the Glory that surrounds Him
So those united in love and harmony
Are enraptured by brilliance of the Glory
of God the Father

Give Glory to God the Son
The Word that spoke creation into being
Who sadly observed the Fall of Adam and Eve
Then willingly consented out of pure love
To save the world from Eternal Damnation
In human and divine nature he walked the Earth
Teaching and spreading seeds of love
Taking root in His apostles whose faithful journey
Accompanied Him to the Cross
that led to the final Glory of the Resurrection
Giving us the hope of Eternal Life
Where we can witness the ultimate King of Glory
Seated on His throne surrounded by an aura
And blinding light that emanates the Glory
Of God the Son

Give Glory to the Mother of God
Mary most Holy
The one chosen to crush the serpent
As filled with faith and love, she answered
Thy will be done
Setting in motion the plan of salvation
And she followed her son to the cross
While she bore the sorrows that pierced her heart
So that all of creation could be free
To choose love and life over sin and death
Receiving Her crown as Queen of Heaven and Earth
She has her place of honor in a cloud of the Glory
Of Mary our Mother

Give glory to God, the Holy Spirit
The breath of Life, the fire of Love
The One who hovers day and night
Waiting for the call of despair
Or the heart that suddenly opens
Anxious to receive the grace and the nudge
To begin the journey and love affair
That leads to the Spouse who patiently waits
For every soul to find its way
To the One who is waiting every day
For the sinner who emerges from his prayer
To acknowledge the gift that is present to him
As he arises filled with the ecstasy and Glory
Of the Holy Spirit

March 2023

MOTHER MARY

Sweet young virgin, so meek and so mild
Said YES to the Angel to fulfill the plan
That God Almighty had in store for man
Pondering all things deep in her heart
Trusting in God's plan from the very start
Mother most holy, Mother most chaste
Fulfilled God's plan for the whole human race.

She conquered the devil with a single word
Her YES won the battle without wielding a sword
As the baby she bore would become Jesus, our Lord
To save the human race from eternal anguish
She did not know what the future would bring
But trusting in God gave her strength to sing
Of the magnificent things the Almighty has done
For her and Elizabeth and everyone
through all the ages under the sun

My soul proclaims the greatness of the Lord,
my spirit rejoices in God my Savior
for he has looked with favor on his lowly servant.
From this day all generations will call me blessed:
the Almighty has done great things for me,
and holy is his Name.

She never wavered but always pondered
All of these things deep in her heart
And she trusted in God
All of her days from the very start

Portraits of Grace

Young as she was, she had no fear
And began the journey that would end in tears
As she would watch her Son stripped bare
And wince as the whips pierced his skin
Dripping with blood and ragged flesh
Torn to pieces until He took His last breath
Her heart felt the sword as it pierced His side
The sorrow was more than a mother could bear
But the Father was with her, in her, through her despair
To hold her and comfort her until the dawn
When Mother most holy, Mary most chaste
Saw the fulfillment of Gods plan for the whole human race

April 2023

RAGING WATERS

The waters are raging around me
The night is shrouded in darkness
My boat is adrift far out at sea
I have no anchor, I cry in distress
I am lost and alone, unable to see
As the fog rolls in and envelopes me
Where am I going, what do I do
I have no direction without you

As I peer through the darkness over the water
I see a glimmer of light far away
And hope springs up that it draws near
To rescue me from my dismay
It seems to come close but then disappears
And I sink in the boat and start to pray
As my mind and soul are shrouded in fear
Will I be left here to perish in this lonely way

Rescue me, please, my Lord and my God
I am lost and alone without direction
I have nowhere to turn, I cry out so loud
But is it in vain, for the answer is lost
As the waves toss me about like a child in a crowd
And then I imagine You upon the cross
Surrounded by darkness and alone left to die

My whimpering stops, as You show me the way
Without words, I know that the answer is Faith
That grows and becomes stronger every day
As we take the time to be still and pray

Then listen in the quiet or the raging sea
For the message that you have especially for me
It may not be loud or given in words
But my heart knows what You want me to hear
And it always will lead me out of my fear
I love You, My Jesus
Amen

April 2023

LOVING JESUS

Mother Mary,
Help me to love your Son
With a heart like yours
That embodies

Angelic Countenance
Beauty of Soul
Compassion and Attentiveness
Depth of Love
Eternal Motherhood/Sisterhood
Faithful follower
Gifted and Grace filled
Heart of Wisdom
Intercessor in Prayer
Joyful Obedience
Keeping all things in your heart
Loving with Abandon
Model of Integrity
Nurturing
Obedient and steadfast
Pure and Pondering
Quiet acceptance
Reaching out to the needy
Suffering Servant
Tapestry of many sorrows
Unwavering in Hope
Virtue overflowing
Welcoming the brokenhearted
Xtraordinary Strength of character
Yearning to be near the Father and Jesus
Zeal for the mission of your Son

And Loving Jesus forever and ever
Amen

April 2023

THE PERFECT GIFT

Not just one gift, but many
A whole package of precious gifts
You've given to me, my precious love
Not deserving, as I'm often adrift
But they're showered upon me from above
Throughout my life to give me a lift
As signs to me of Your true love

First there is the gift of Life
Given in grace through the fruit of marriage
As my mother and father, husband and wife
Waited for years to fill the carriage
That they would stroll with delight
Loving and nurturing along the way
As my life blossomed in love every day

The next gift was a similar gift of Life,
As at my Baptism, I became a child of God
Filled with the Spirit and anointed with oil
The seal was stamped on my soul
That forever and ever I would always be
His child for all eternity
Through life and death forever more
His glorious presence I will adore

Portraits of Grace

Then another gift came my way,
Cleansed by Confession, receiving His grace
I felt so pure and close to Him
on my First Communion Day
Dressed all in white as a Bride in her gown
Receiving Him into my body
I am fed by Him nearly every day
Never to be parted, always in love
For this I fervently pray

The gifts keep on coming as His bounty is endless
A match made in Heaven He gave to me
When I met my sweet love, not by chance
But obviously planned from before we were born
As seldom a marriage so perfect and smooth
Growing in love with every day
We are filled with joy as we work and play
Thankful for these gifts in every way

As we immersed ourselves in His loving arms
Nurturing our faith that would shield us from harm
And the blessings continued, our children were born
Precious gifts, each unique and special one
Filling our lives with joy and delight
Teaching us at times how to deal with strife
As we turned to Him to lead the way
And receive the grace needed each day
To teach and nurture, love and pray
Our family, symbol of love and unity

Amidst this time, other gifts were showered
As our communities expanded year by year
With Friendships and prayer groups
Sharing and caring, helping and serving
Talents blossomed, another gift from Heaven above
As we continue to share these gifts and our love
His presence immersed in all that we do
As daily we give thanks for joy so true

The last gift we will receive is not a mortal ending
As Death is but a new Life just beginning
The perfect gift opened by the death of our Lord
So we could be with Him for all eternity
Where forever in His presence we will be
Thus He leads the way to our very last breath
No longer meandering or adrift
He's given us the perfect life, the perfect gift

April 2023

INTO HIS ARMS

Into His arms you will be received
On the day that He calls you home
And you will reach out to Him
With a smile on your face and hope in your heart
Your eyes connect and He searches your soul
Finding beauty and love and a deep desire
To be with Him now and forever

He will hold you and carry your tired body
To its Heavenly home to rest and be restored
He has prepared a place for you near to Him
That is surrounded by beauty and peace
And as He settles you into your new home
You begin to relax and find joy again
As you watch Him thru the clouds ascend to His throne

And as He takes His seat, His glory abounds
with brilliant golden rays spread out into eternity
As myriads of angels fill the space
With song and praise, worship and grace
For the One who redeemed you and the whole human race
From sin and poverty, doubt and disgrace
So you could one day call Heaven your home
And forever rest with Him in this place

March 2023

FAITH

Faith builds on a foundation of prayer
In the light of day or dark of night
In a chapel, church or anywhere
We open our hearts to get insight
On stripping our soul until it is bare
Waiting for a word as we kneel in prayer
That shields us from the threat of despair
PATIENCE

The power of that Word is so great
That the anticipation of it lifts us high
But the danger may be that we must wait
According to His will for when it is right
For the message to be revealed in His time
So the fullness of it will come to light
And we recognize it as inspired and divine
HOPE

Little by little there are a few signs
Of His presence and nearness that ease the mind
And give me hope of His love divine
To pacify me and keep me in line
As I wait for the answer in the fulfillment of time
For He knows how much I need to grow
Before I am ready to accept His will
For what must come next
OPENNESS

Portraits of Grace

Wide open, tender and vulnerable
Yet wielding a sword of courage
Given to me by the Spirit himself
I dare not retreat as He lifts the veil
Emerging from prayer with confidence
Ready for the battle to begin
Covered in the armor of love
I am ready to conquer and win
TRUST

Again, the Spirit moves and nudges me
Be bold, be strong, we are one
I will be with you until all is done
The time is now, take the leap
Jump off the mountain into my Hand
I will carry you across the chasm
You will not fall, so enjoy the ride
As I carry you to the other side
FAITH

The battle is over, the day is done
A sigh of relief as we have won
At least for today, I can rest
With no worry of failing the test
For He is with me every day
And lifts me up as I pray
To receive the kiss from above
That settles my soul with true love
PEACE

April 2023

HOLY TRINITY

God, the Father
Creator of Heaven and Earth
In your abounding Wisdom
All things have known rebirth
Forgiving all my sins
Through You I have life
Fill me with radiating joy
A reflection of Your great Glory

Jesus Christ, my Savior
With You I have hope
Looking past my stubborn will
You show me Your face
Eyes piercing me with love
And not a sign of disgrace
Admonishing my sin
as You hold me in Your arms
Promising me a Home with You
Forever in Heaven above

Holy Spirit, you are my Guide
Through you I have Faith
Fill me with your peace
Watch over me with love
Protect me from all harm
Be always with me
And shelter me from storms
You whisper in my ear
The words I need to hear
I can always count on You
To release the clutch of fear

Holy Trinity
A union of three persons
Magnificent, powerful, glorified
The Father, Son and Holy Spirit
The three are also One
A mystery from the beginning
As God the Father spoke the Word of Creation
Jesus was that Word that brought it about
And the Spirit was the breath
that filled the Earth with Life

The Trinity
Like three circles that stand alone
Yet overlapping and linking one another
A union that cannot be broken
Each bringing its own dimension
That reaches into creation in its own way

Fill me with your endless love

April 2023

RAYS OF GLORY

Rays of glory and splendor
Emanate in every direction
Reaching out to all of Creation
That You have spoken into being
Touching those waiting and watching
For signs of Your presence
Drifting around those without a clue
Who do not yet recognize You

You are Lord of the Universe
Ruler of the World
Lover of all creatures great and small
Providing for all our needs
Keeping us safe as You heed the call
Of those bowed down in humble prayer
As well as those who are unaware
Or desperately caught in an evil lair

Pouring out graces upon us all
Landing on those who reach out to You
Letting them fill their empty heart
With blessings that give them comfort
Then slowly stirring their senses
Into a whirlpool of emotion
Radiating God's glory deep in their soul
That leads them to love and charity

As love, joy and peace
Overcome our aberrant nature
And our eyes are opened
To see the King of Creation
Holding out the Lamb of Salvation
To those who reach out to receive
The most precious gift of all
We're transformed into a new creation
Amid His rays of Glory

April 2023

PATIENCE, MY LOVE

Deep in my chair
Where seldom is heard
The sound of Your voice
But waiting in darkness
To know You are near
I've learned to be patient
And not to fear
As eventually
a hint of Your presence
Will begin to appear

But even if not
No longer shedding a tear
Or pouting like a child
Not getting her way
I remain still and quiet
And without a word
I pray for the nearness of You
To strengthen and fill me
Inspire and love me

A little while longer
There in the distance
May just be a hint
So far away, I need to squint
A tiny point of light
Atop a slender column of white
Maybe a candle beyond my sight
Come closer to me I pray
So I can feel and see You today
Or hear what You want to say

And as I wait patiently
The light does move toward me
A circle of yellow appears above
The approaching column of white
Slow and steady comes the light
On the edge of my chair, I get ready
For the vision to burst in full view
As I realize without any demise
It's truly a vision of You
With a halo round your head
In a garment of white
And Your arms stretched out
As You did on the cross
With the love that astounds me
Now ready to surround me
With Your presence and love
Calm as the peace of a dove
From Heaven above
And I am rewarded for
Patience, My Love

May 2023

LOVE LETTERS

Love letters from days of yore
I treasure still as I did before
Sensing Your touch in words you spoke
As a yearning in me they would evoke
Feeling the warmth run thru my veins
Knowing my life wouldn't be the same
I come to you with expectant hope
As I quiet in prayer and release the yoke
Of worldly burdens that strain and choke
Letter of Prayer

Not only words you've whispered in my ear
But those you've recorded for all to hear
Stimulate the senses and move the heart
So that desire grows that we never part
As I read the words on the written page
They will be with me always through the ages
It comes to life in such a fashion
That I am overwhelmed with much passion
Letter of the Word

And the Spirit moves throughout the day
Having a multitude of things to say
A piece of advice, a nudge to reach out
He's always near dropping letters about
Smile and share peace, pray for this world
Open your heart to the hurting soul

Portraits of Grace

Kind deeds, warm hugs, opportunities untold
To be the heart and hands of the Spirit so bold
If we open our ears to His constant chatter
He will touch us so our love will be scattered
Letter of the Spirit

Then comes the most intimate letter of all
Where my love gives all of himself to me
I don't even wait for the sound of His call
For in Him and near Him I want to be
I yearn for His body with great expectation
For the moment that I receive Him into me
That we may be one to create a new Life
And forever shed that which creates strife
The sin and the darkness that lurks about
Replaced with love that makes me shout
As tears of joy and thanks flow in a stream
I know this is real and not a dream
Letter of the Eucharist

I cherish all my letters
And read them one by one
At a very special time and
In a very special place
As often as I can
Which is almost every day
Because I go to Mass
Where these letters come anew
As I kneel to pray and hear His word
And let the Spirit guide my soul
Change me and renew me
Through the Body of Christ
Letter of the Mass

Put it all together and
You have the final letter
The one revealed in Heaven
As the Supper of the Lamb
And we partake on Earth
As often as we can
For no greater love than this
Can be shared with anyone
As the heavenly choir of angels
Surround each and every one
Who receives the bread of Heaven
Upon his hungry tongue

My collection of love letters so dear
Continues to grow with each year
As the time we spend together
Evokes new feelings and emotions
New revelations and intimate devotions
It will not end, not even on the last day
But continue in Heaven, for this I pray
Eternal Love Letters
(My personal collection)

April 2023

POEMS FOR MY GRANDCHILDREN

MY EASTER LILY

Lily of the Valley
So pure and so bright
Your sweet aroma fills the air
Through the day and through the night

A vision of loveliness
A beauty to behold
A gift for the eyes
Beyond any ever told

Though the winds may rage around
You stand ever firm and tall
Though swaying in the storm
You will never fall

Always pointing towards Heaven
Your petals reach for its height
The grace of God surrounds you
As you grow in His light

As the day fades away
And night draws near
Your petals fold together
To hold your love so dear

You will always be my Lily
So pure and so white
Bringing joy to my life
Filling us all with delight

Portraits of Grace

March 2021

MY ZOË MAE

As you wake in the morning
Laughter in your eyes
Sunshine on your face
Just a glimpse of you
Fills my heart with grace

Full of imagination
You are an amazing
 Work of God's creation
Always ready for something new
Searching through life for what is true

Ever ready for adventure
Watchful eyes, keen perception
Always in search of treasures
To add to your collection
Rocks, flowers, leaves, feathers
You gather together for protection

Intrigued by the variety in nature
You've got a plethora of knowledge
About a multitude of creatures
Always learning something new
Sharing it later with those around you.

But so well rounded are you, my child,
The outdoors is not your only forté
You're just as happy in the kitchen
Helping to chop, stir and sauté
Yummy food to please the palate

Also, loving games and all sorts of crafts
Being creative is one of your knacks
There is none like my Zoë Mae
A marvel, unique, pretty and bold
Stories of you will forever be told.

July 2021

EMMITT

Emmitt James Lemaire
No one would ever dare
To call you dull and boring
As most of the time you are soaring
Full of energy and love of life
Ordinary things inspire such delight.

Bold and fearless most of the time,
Strong and confident, with valiance you shine
Yet gentle and caring, you can also be
With love and compassion for family
Your enthusiasm is contagious to those around you
Helping lift spirits in those who are blue.

A grin often covers your face, ear to ear
Showing your heart to everyone near
Not a stranger you know, though never met
You greet them with gusto and welcoming net
Drawing them to you as friends forever
Your love for people shines in all your endeavors

Sitting and reading is one of your passions
As learning and creating are also your fashion
While pretending takes us to worlds unknown
As your wild imagination has often shown
From a trip to the doctor, to the moon we zoom
Then stuck on a planet in a laboratory room

Watching you grow is my privilege and delight
As is playing, praying and kissing you goodnight

Portraits of Grace

The world through your eyes makes me young at heart
And I hope through the years, we are seldom apart
I wish you the best, my Emmitt, with love
That Heaven pours graces on you from above.

December 2021

AUTUMN RENEÉ

Autumn, my sweet girl
Radiant as the colors of the season
Beautiful to behold
Intriguing and spontaneous
Changing like the wind

Brilliant like the Yellow sun
Full of energy and so much fun
Diligence is one of your attributes
Perfecting skills before your time
Demonstrating your sharp mind

Glowing with the allure of Orange embers
Cherishing the warmth of a snuggly hug
The strings of my heart feel a tug
As the smile on your face spreads to a grin
And your beautiful blue eyes beckon within

Alluring at times with your Golden glow
Beckoning with the sparkle in your eye
Challenging the beholder with your impish grin
Only you know what's running through your mind
As you dart away to begin the chase

Bold and confident you take your stand
Not to be conquered by any in the land
Then sudden laughter from deep within
As you fall to the ground for the win
Never a Fall yet or to come
Like our Autumn whose colors abound

November 2021

MEYER JOHN

I know a boy who's turning One
He is so cute and so much fun
If you should happen to walk by,
With a twinkle in his eye,
A smile will spread across his face
Until his body can't stay in place
And he begins to talk and coo
Just out of sheer delight in you.

Observant and quiet has been his nature
Content to watch all around him
Slowly trying a thing or two
Not anxious to join the Lemaire Zoo
But as he approaches his special day,
He is starting to learn how to play,
To crawl and climb and toddle along,
Even dancing to many a song.
Look out world here he comes,
Our little boy Meyer John

July 2021

MIRACLE OF LIFE – NATALIE

Sweet little baby
Born of True Love
Surrounded by angels
From Heaven above

Innocent and pure
You come as a gift
Always to cherish
And thankfully uplift

You're born to a family
Who loves you so much,
Waiting to hold you, kiss you
And make a big fuss

So glad you are here
In the arms of your Mom
Who'll hold you so dear
For hours to come

You'll melt your Dad's heart
As you gaze in his eyes
And he'll cherish you forever
So don't be surprised

But Autumn, your big sister
Has been waiting so long
She'll be your first friend
And help you toddle along

The angels watch over you
And keep you safe in the night
While we thank the Lord God
For this miracle of Life

January 2022

LOVELY LILY

Updated to 2023

My Easter Lily from days of yore
Continues blossoming each spring
More Beautiful than before
Her radiant colors seem to sing
With brilliant vibrant tones
Changing like a butterfly's wings
As they emerge from the cocoon
A vision of splendor to behold
And a lifelong story to be told

The chapter she writes
at this moment in time
Is either filled with passion
or quietly sublime
She loves to read and write stories
That no one finds boring
Or create magnificent artwork
With imagination that's soaring

Her talents unfold with every year
With Drama and dance the focus today
Or creating stories and costumes
For unique characters in a play
As well as a multitude of friends
That she likes to spend time with
Planning, playing, laughing up a storm
What girls do til the sound of the alarm

Portraits of Grace

But at the end of the day
She is still my Lily
That melts my heart and keeps me young
As we share good times of shopping fun
Born to be the first to say- I love you, Mimi
Through hours of dancing and crafting
Games and creativity
As I watch her grow and blossom
Into my Lovely Lily

Phyllis Comeaux
April 2023

ABOUT THE AUTHOR

Born and raised in South Louisiana, and a life-long Roman Catholic, Phyllis constantly seeks a closer relationship with her Lord. She is committed to her Spiritual formation and growing deeper in the love and service that stem from the fruits of her daily Mass, prayer time and adoration. She is thankful to her parents, grandparents, godparents as true examples of trust and faith in God and their unwavering commitment to being faithful in prayer and practicing their Catholic faith.

Phyllis' true journey started as a young Mom, volunteering to be a catechism teacher for preschoolers, then following their growth by becoming a Scout Religious Award facilitator through all levels. The training and formation required by the Diocese of San Angelo, where her children mostly grew up, was very thorough and life changing in many ways because of the depth and breadth of the program and probably, through the prompting of the Holy Spirit, her readiness to become fully immersed in Spiritual formation and experiencing moving spiritual encounters at times. Since then, many Bible studies, prayer groups, St Joseph Abbey retreats, ACTS retreats, other ministries, etc. have continued to keep the fire lit. So, the yearning has never stopped and never will, as she knows the journey is not over until she meets her Bridegroom in Heaven, when He calls her home and He adorns her in her wedding gown of dazzling white.

www.ingramcontent.com/pod-product-compliance
Lightning Source LLC
Chambersburg PA
CBHW051637050426

42443CB00025B/427